# Brisbane

## A U S T R A L I A

Steve Parish

# DISCOVERING BRISBANE

Unshackled from its stark beginnings as a penal outpost, Brisbane has become the thriving capital city of Queensland. The lazy meanderings of the Brisbane River reflect a friendly, cosmopolitan city that makes the most of its subtropical climate. Alfresco dining, riverside promenades, leafy suburbs and shady verandahs are all part of the city's unhurried lifestyle.

Forested hills and an island-dotted bay complement Brisbane's urban pleasures. A wealth of attractions in the hinterland lie within easy reach of the city — behind the superb coastline of rocky foreshores and sweeping beaches sits a wonderland of volcanic peaks, hidden valleys, lush forests and rich farmland.

**Title Page:**
The iconic "Queenslander" style of house.

**Opposite:**
A ferry passes Eagle Street Pier and finance precinct.

**Left:**
A CityCat rounds Gardens Point on the Town Reach of the Brisbane River.

# QUEEN STREET MALL

Brisbane's retail heart lies beneath the shade canopies and flowering trees of Queen Street Mall. Cinemas, specialty shops and multi-level arcades offer shopping and entertainment seven days a week. Buskers, and staged and impromptu performances bring a festive air to the central meeting place of Brisbane. Park benches and sidewalk cafés invite shoppers to relax and watch the passing parade.

**Right and opposite, above:** Queen Street Mall.

**Opposite, below:** The Queen Street entrance to the Treasury Casino.

**Pages 6–7:** Kangaroo Point and the Story Bridge with Brisbane city (beyond) and New Farm (foreground).

# DAWN AND DUSK

Ever-changing light quality transforms views of the city from dawn to dusk. As night descends, the reflected lights of glittering towers dance across the river.

**Opposite:**
The Brisbane River reflects the city's illuminated beauty at night.

**Left:**
Brisbane city gilded by sunlight.

**Pages 10–11:**
River*fire*, part of the annual River*festival*, lights up the river and the Story Bridge, which links Kangaroo Point and Petrie Bight.

# BRISBANE'S HERITAGE

Numerous heritage trails that weave through Brisbane's streets and riverfront provide fascinating glimpses of Brisbane's first one hundred years. An excellent boardwalk now marks the site of the timber wharves where passengers and cargo arrived in the new colony. Commercial and public squares, spired churches, and commercial and government buildings display an array of architectural styles ranging from the Georgian simplicity of the convict-built Commissariat Stores to the classical lines of the Shrine of Remembrance at Anzac Square.

**Right:**
The Old Mill on Wickham Terrace was originally powered by a convict treadmill.

**Opposite:**
From Central Station's clock tower to Anzac and Post Office Squares.

**Pages 14–15:**
The beach at South Bank is the perfect place to cool down.

# SOUTH BANK PARKLANDS

South Bank Parklands is a delightful oasis just a short stroll from the city centre. It is a great place to walk, cycle, enjoy a meal, take a swim or catch a lift on a river ferry or CityCat. Outdoor concerts and weekend markets draw crowds of pleasure-seekers.

The marvellous exhibits and collections of the State's museum, library and art gallery can be found at the nearby Queensland Cultural Centre, which is also home to the Performing Arts Complex.

**Opposite:**
South Bank at night with the CityCat jetty at front.

**Left:**
Visitors stroll along the bougainvillea-covered Arbour.

**Pages 18–19:**
Eagle Street Pier and Riverside Centre precinct.

# RIVERSIDE CENTRE

The Riverside Centre is the hub of Brisbane's financial precinct. After dark and on weekends, it shakes off the sobriety of business to become a lively gathering spot. A variety of nightclubs, bistros and restaurants cater to all tastes. On Sundays, craft and clothing stalls crowd the plazas and riverside walkways. The paddlewheelers and ferries that operate from Eagle Street Pier offer river tours of Brisbane.

**Right:**
Eagle Street Pier
and Riverside
Centre.

**Opposite:**
The *River
Queen II* at
Eagle Street
Pier.

# JACARANDA TIME

Brisbane has embraced this beautiful tree as its unofficial floral emblem. Each spring, city parks and suburban gardens blaze with the intense colour of jacaranda flowers. Fallen blossoms carpet the ground as the tree's feathery leaves begin to emerge. The avenue of jacarandas at New Farm Park creates one of the city's most striking floral displays.

**Opposite:** Spring arrives in the city by the Botanic Gardens.

**Left:** A carpet of blossoms at New Farm Park.

# THE QUEENSLANDER

Brisbane has many fine examples of the State's unique housing
style known as "The Queenslander". Designed to lessen the
effects of cyclones and humid summers, these timber houses
sit high above the ground on tin-capped hardwood stumps.
High ceilings and deep verandahs help cool the interior, while
hallways and windows channel breezes. Many proud owners
lovingly restore 19th-century houses, while reproductions of
their grace and charm are often built.

**Right:**
Ridge-top
Queenslanders
catch the
summer breeze.

**Opposite:**
Across the roofs
of Paddington to
Mt Coot-tha.

# SUBURBAN HOSPITALITY

Brisbane's inner suburbs host a vibrant social scene that revolves around cafés, pubs, art galleries and bookshops. The wrought-iron verandahs and cool high rooms of traditional venues like the Regatta Hotel are specially loved, even as they compete with the casual clean lines of contemporary eating establishments.

**Opposite:**
The Regatta Hotel on the Toowong Reach of the Brisbane River.

**Left:**
The café scene at Park Road, Milton.

# MT COOT-THA

The scenic drive winding up the forested slopes of Mt Coot-tha leads to a remarkable panorama of coastal South-East Queensland. On a clear day, the view sweeps from the peaks of the border ranges across the city to Moreton Bay and northwards to the intriguingly-shaped Glass House Mountains. Mt Coot-tha's walking tracks, picnic grounds and 52-hectare Botanic Gardens make it an ideal location for family outings.

**Right:**
The city viewed from Mt Coot-tha.

**Opposite:**
The lookout on top of Mt Coot-tha.

# BRISBANE FOREST PARK

This magnificent reserve of natural bush stretches north from Mt Coot-tha along the D'Aguilar Range. It encompasses 28,500 hectares of city parkland, national park and State forest. Visitors can explore the park by car or bicycle, on horseback or on foot.

Its eucalypt forest, open woodland and subtropical rainforest offer an endless variety of outdoor pastimes. Encounters with native wildlife are common, and spring wildflowers bring a special beauty to this richly diverse stretch of bush.

**Opposite:**
A quiet moment in Maiala National Park.

**Left:**
An Orange-eyed Tree-frog, one of the park's native inhabitants.

# INDEX

**Right:**
The city viewed
from the
City Botanic
Gardens.